Puerto Rico

Steve Simonsen

 Pisces Books®
A division of Gulf Publishing Company
Houston, Texas

ACKNOWLEDGMENTS

I would like to thank the Puerto Rican Department of Tourism and the following dive operators:

Aquatic Underwater Adventures
Blue Caribe Dive Center
Capt. Bill's Dive Shop
Coral Head Divers
Culebra Dive Shop
Parguera Divers
Solimar Divers

And I would like to thank my lovely wife Janet Simonsen who deciphered my handwriting and typed the original manuscript.

♣ **Pisces Books®**
A division of Gulf Publishing Company
P.O. Box 2608
Houston, Texas 77252-2608

Pisces Books is a registered trademark of Gulf Publishing Company.

Printed in Hong Kong

10   9   8   7   6   5   4   3   2   1

Library of Congress Cataloging-in-Publication Data
Simonsen, Steve.
    Diving and snorkeling guide to Puerto Rico / Steve Simonsen.
        p.   cm.
    Includes index.
    ISBN 1-55992-084-X
        1. Deep diving—Puerto Rico—Guidebooks.   2. Skin diving—
    Puerto Rico—Guidebooks.   3. Puerto Rico—Guidebooks.   I.
    Title.
    GV840.S78S55 1996
    797.2'3—dc20   95-21437
                                                        CIP

Table of Contents

How to Use This Guide

This guide is intended to show a sampling of dive sites and conditions typical of diving in Puerto Rico. The island is as big as the state of Connecticut. To say that the book covers all of Puerto Rico would be unfair.

Perhaps what is best about diving in Puerto Rico is that the dive operators themselves share in the adventure and routinely make new discoveries that may or may not appear in print, and possibly will not even have a name.

Geographical areas are treated separately. The guide begins with the islands of Vieques and Culebra and travels clockwise ending with the island of Desecheo. The east, southwest, and west are covered. The north shore was omitted intentionally because it is highly seasonal.

Beach diving is popular in the northwest and there are big caves near Isabela. With the arrival of cooler winter weather the north swell invades calm beach sites and surfers start spreading wax on their boards.

The clearest water is usually several miles offshore and that is where most of the diving takes place.

The Rating System for Dives and Divers

Each site was given one or two ratings. The ratings are novice, intermediate, and advanced.

A *novice diver* is one who is recently certified at entry level and has made 1–25 dives. An *intermediate diver* is someone who has more than 25 dives, takes one or more dive trips each year and may have participated in some form of continuing diver education programs. An *advanced diver* generally has been diving for more than 2 years, has executed 50 or more dives and is comfortable in most ocean conditions.

The ocean has a powerful way of humbling humans, and certification cards do not always reflect the evident level of diver expertise.

1

Overview of Puerto Rico

History

Settled by indigenous groups for thousands of years before the arrival of Columbus in 1493, Puerto Rico was a Spanish colony for four centuries with early military preoccupations replaced by agricultural and economical concerns by the 19th century. Since 1893, it has been under United States sovereignty, providing Puerto Ricans with U.S. citizenship. In 1952, Puerto Rico ratified its own constitution, which created the Commonwealth of Puerto Rico.

Visitors today see an island with a population of 3.7 million, a place where time present and time past mingle in the shape of old Spanish forts and modern high-rises.

The people, together with the sea, extend a hospitable welcome with open arms.

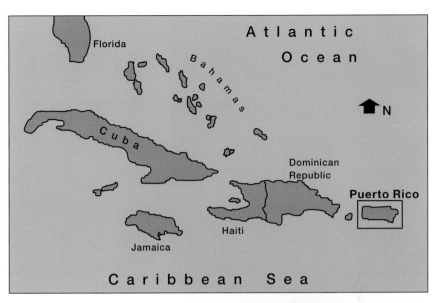

The sense of family is big among Puerto Ricans and their willingness to communicate and welcome travelers to their island is comforting for anyone away from home. ▶

◀ The turrets that once guarded the fort in old San Juan now welcome visitors to the historic fortress of El Morro.

The Punta Higuera lighthouse, near Rincon, was built in 1892, damaged by an earthquake in 1918, and then rebuilt in 1921. Now it is fully operational and stands as a landmark to the best surfing in Puerto Rico.

Besides the larger islands of Culebra and Vieques, there are many smaller uninhabited islands between Puerto Rico and the United States Virgin Islands to the east. ▶

Highway 10 connects the two cities of Arecibo, to the north, and Ponce, on the south. It crosses the Cordillera central and winds its way through rich tropical rain forest.

Geography

Puerto Rico is 1,000 miles southeast of Miami and is about 110 miles long and 35 miles wide, roughly the shape of Connecticut. The terrain ranges from palm-lined beaches spread over 270 miles of coastline to verdant rain forests and mountain ranges reaching 4,390 feet high. The southwest is dry, desert-like, and home to more species of birds than anywhere else in Puerto Rico.

Puerto Rico is truly an island rich in contrasts, such as dry rolling hills in the southwest and lush tropical rain forests in the northeast.

Driving through El Yunque Rain Forest near San Juan allows visitors a close-up look at the only tropical rain forest in the U.S. Forest Service. Hiking on trails or driving brings one to waterfalls and huge stands of bamboo and along winding roads that ascend through misty mountain jungles with more than 240 tree species.

Old forts, Spanish architecture, and fabulous restaurants make a half-day or night spent in Old San Juan a cultural experience equal to traveling to Spain and the Mediterranean. A visitor can drive from San Juan to just about anywhere in about three hours. A scenic highway runs from Tuna Point (Manaubo) across to Mayaguez.

West of Ponce—named after Puerto Rico's first explorer, Juan Ponce De Leon—in the hills surrounding Guanica, is the world's largest tract of dry, tropical, coastal forest. These low-lying hills are now a part of an international biosphere reserve and one of 20 designated forest reserves throughout Puerto Rico.

In the northwest near Arecibo, home of the world's largest radio telescope, the Camuy River vanishes into the blue hole near the town of Lares. Spectacular sink holes descend 170 feet. Trams, walkways, or stairs can be taken to explore some of the many caves in the Karst limestone region.

Along the east coast, from Fajardo to Humacao, are two of the island's largest resorts, with an astonishing array of amenities including golf courses and watersports facilities.

Two favorite pastime activities of the Puerto Ricans are fishing and baseball.

2

Diving in Puerto Rico

The climate is tropical, with the average air temperature of 82°F (28°C) and constant easterly tradewinds. Ocean temperature ranges from 77°–84°F. Experienced divers prefer using full, lightweight wetsuits or shorties in winter and a dive skin or bathing suit alone during the summer months.

The underwater visibility averages 60 to 75 feet. Near shore and under certain conditions, visibility can drop to near 30 feet, while generally offshore the water is beautifully clear, 100 feet or better.

Much of the best diving, for that reason alone, is done several miles offshore. Dive operators throughout Puerto Rico all seem to share a love for boats and do not mind making longer trips to reach better sites. Divers, on the other hand, unfamiliar with the motion of the ocean can be vulnerable to seasickness. Precautions for those individuals should be taken.

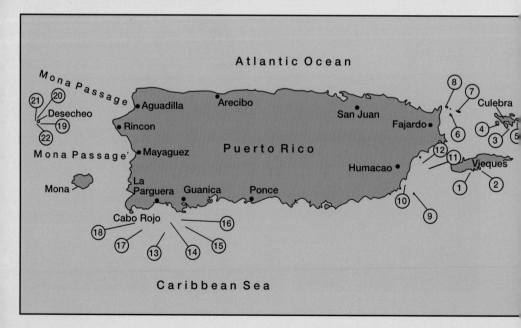

Most dive boats carry small groups of six or more and one is likely to be diving with the owner of the shop in most cases. Along with their love for boats, their sense of adventure has not been lost after years of successful operation. New dive sites are constantly being discovered and given names along with an entry in the log book of the GPS (Global Positioning System) coordinates.

The north shore of Puerto Rico has not been acclaimed for world-class diving, but there are popular diving areas off of San Juan that sport over-

Dive Site Ratings	Novice	Intermediate	Advanced
Vieques Island			
1 Angel Reef	X	X	X
2 Patti's Reef	X	X	X
Culebra Island*			
3 Amberjack		X	X
4 Cayo Raton		X	X
5 Tug Boat		X	X
Eastern Puerto Rico			
6 Palomenitos*	X	X	X
7 Diablo	X	X	X
8 Cayo Lobos	X	X	X
9 The Reserve		X	X
10 The Cracks	X	X	X
11 Whoville		X	X
12 The Drift	X	X	X
La Parguera			
13 Black Wall		X	X
14 Barracuda City	X	X	X
15 The Buoy		X	X
16 1990	X	X	X
17 High Light		X	X
18 The Motor	X	X	X
Desecheo			
19 Candyland		X	X
20 Yellow Reef		X	X
21 Puerto de Botes		X	X
22 Candlesticks		X	X

*Indicates excellent snorkeling sites.

hangs, tunnels, lava tubes, and caves. Surprisingly enough, the marine critters include flying gurnards, arrow crabs, octopus, and tiny sea horses.

While boat diving is the norm, there are sections of the northwest coast near Isabela and Aguadilla that offer shore diving. Winter waves along the north can limit access and reduce visibility, but a bad day of diving still beats a good day of work.

Puerto Rico is linked by an undersea plateau and many smaller islands and cays with the Virgin Islands to the east. The diving is done on colorful fringing reefs that rarely dip below 80 feet with average depths of 50 and 60 feet.

Long Snout Sea Horses

These strangely shaped fish have reportedly been found along the north shore of the island in shallow water. Belonging to the same family (Synenathidae) as pipefish, the delicate body of the seahorse resembles the chess knight. The use of their prehensile tails allows them to coil around rope sponges, sea grass and other holdfasts. Unlike pipefish that swim horizontally, seahorses swim upright using only dorsal and pectoral fins and deploy a combination of color, texture and motion to remain largely undetected by predators. They feed primarily on planktonic crustaceans.

The breeding habits are most noteworthy because the females turn over the eggs to the males to be incubated in the pouch for about six weeks. The male often rubs or scratches his pouch against something to encourage the youngsters out. With this stimulation, as many as 100 tiny seahorses disperse and begin feeding on tiny crustaceans immediately.

Near the southeast, the continental size of things shapes up with deeper diving and clearer water with generally 80- to 100-foot visibility. Famous for its Phosphorescent Bay, the area of La Parguera on the southwest coast offers the most spectacular walls on the island.

Along the placid west coast, there is diving near shore but for big adventure, divers make arrangements to visit the legendary Desecheo Island west of Rincon or schedule a diving and camping excursion to the remote Mona Island, 50 miles west of Mayaguez.

There are more than eighty flights each day arriving in Puerto Rico and diving can be arranged either from luxury five-star resorts or a network of paradores, which are hotels that offer reasonably priced accommodations near places of natural or historical interest. Paradores are not for those who expect elegantly appointed rooms and chocolates on their pillow at night. Rather, they are for those who like sports and want a clean room and a chance to meet the people of Puerto Rico and enjoy their local customs.

Unlike some countries, there is no problem with the drinking water and visitors have all the conveniences associated with lifestyles of "The States."

◀ *These fisherman of Rincon provide a rare glimpse of the seldom seen Mahogany snapper.*

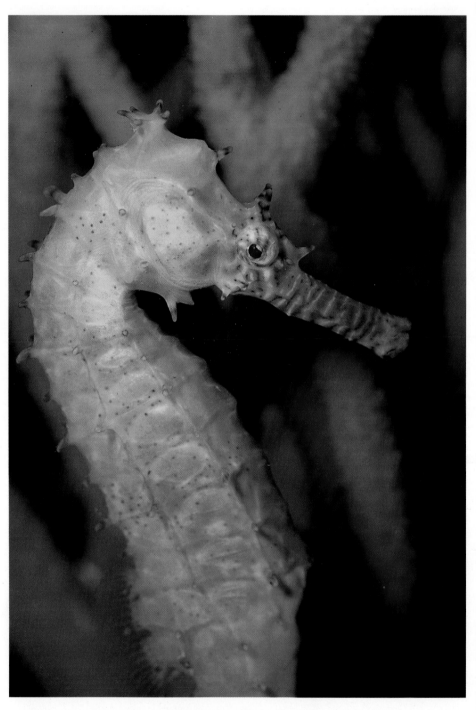

Seahorses' heads are bent sharply down and their prehensile tails are usually wrapped around vertically oriented seagrass or sponges for purposes of concealment.

3

Diving in Vieques

The island of Vieques is situated several miles from the eastern tip of Puerto Rico in the Vieques Passage, which separates Puerto Rico from the U.S. Virgin Islands. It can be reached by small plane from Fajardo or San Juan in 15 or 20 minutes and is serviced twice daily by a passenger ferry out of Fajardo that takes a little over one hour.

This sleepy getaway island is 30 miles long, with 9,000 friendly neighbors of Taino Indian, Spanish, African, Danish, French, British, and U.S. descent. The people are easygoing, slow to anger, and very tolerant. The town of Isabel Segunda resembles a Latin American town straight from the 1950s—right down to the old-fashioned barber shop pole.

There are dozens of truly secluded beaches, shell grounds, mangrove lagoons, and coral reefs, yet the island remains largely undisturbed by development and tourism. This is probably due to the presence of two

The mangrove lagoon serves as a nursery for many young reef fish including miniature barracudas.

Traveling up the closed polyped stalks of giant sea rods are two flamingo tongue snails.

U.S. naval maneuver areas on each end of the island. Even though there are few military personnel, the island is periodically used by the U.S. Navy for combat exercises including bombing.

While Vieques is not noted for its urban night life, there is a phenomenal nightly display of bioluminescence in the mangrove bay near the south shore town of Esperanza. Early each night, spectators arrive in small boats or kayaks to marvel at the concentration of millions of micro-organisms known as dinoflagellates. These give off a ghostly blue-green glow whenever the water is stirred up by a boat, oars, hands or any movement, including rain. This display is best seen on moonless nights and occurs every night of the year. The cosmic shooting trails left behind from fish fleeing the oncoming boat, along with the glowing silhouette of a southern ray gliding silently over the shallow bottom and the sky full of stars overhead, help create an unforgettable evening.

There are only a handful of these remarkable bays in the world, and Puerto Rico is blessed with two of them; the other one is near the seaside community of La Parguera. Pollution and construction will destroy them and lights will diminish the effect; therefore, Puerto Rico is working to protect these shining seas.

Generally referred to as sea fans or gorgonians, these soft corals cover miles and miles of reef areas and orient their interconnected net-like branches perpendicular to surge and wave direction.

The combination of yellow wrasse, coral, and sponges can compose beautiful reef scenes that are artistically painted with a sudden flash of light.

Typical depth range:	40–60 feet
Typical current conditions:	Slight to none
Expertise required:	Novice
Access:	Boat

Along the southern coast west of Esperanza, a short 20- or 30- minute boat ride puts you on top of Angel Reef. A mile or more off shore, the dive operators use a small hand-held GPS (Global Positioning System) to pinpoint the reef location.

Here, spur and groove formations run perpendicular to shore and the reef top is 40 feet deep. The top is covered in gently swaying soft corals, mostly giant sea rods and lavender Venus sea fans. There are two Spanish anchors, one on top and one at the base of the reef face in 60 feet of water. These anchors are deeply embedded into the coral and are pointed out to divers by the divemaster. Where the reef drops steeply to join a large white sand channel, yellow wrasses swim quickly along the edge. Schools of grey angelfish are present here and the visibility is 50 to 60 feet. The surface can be a bit bumpy, but underwater there is little or no current.

Fast swimmers, the bluehead wrasse seen here in both the initial and terminal phase may act as cleaners by removing parasites from larger fish.

Patti's Reef

Typical depth range:	20–40 feet
Typical current conditions:	Mild current, big surge
Expertise required:	Novice
Access:	Boat

Closer to the reef crest and within site of the buildings of Esperanza, Patti's Reef is a nice sun-drenched series of heavy sand channels. Formed among massive elkhorn coral and spires of boulder star coral, the undersides and edges are laced with bright orange icing sponges. The more delicate staghorn corals favor the shallow 20- to 40- foot reef top. The bases of the ancient coral reef have numerous cavities, holes, and crevices that house a surprising number of inhabitants including nurse sharks, small, quick red-spotted hawkfish, and tight schools of flattened football-shaped doctorfish. Pelagics such as mackerel cruise in from nearby deeper water and prehistoric-looking sand divers can be seen lying on the bottom with their mouths slightly open revealing shining sharp teeth. In the flick of a tail, they disappear and settle again on the bottom not too far away.

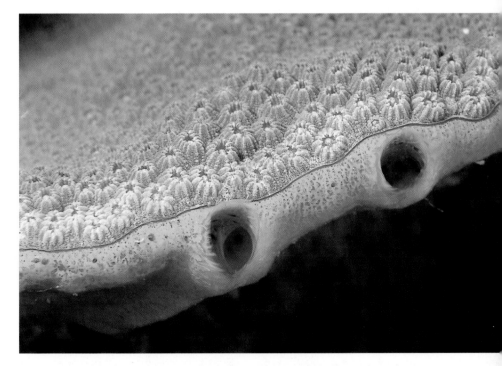

Much of the mound and boulder coral is protected from sponges that bore into the coral by other sponges that simply encrust the margin of coral plates.

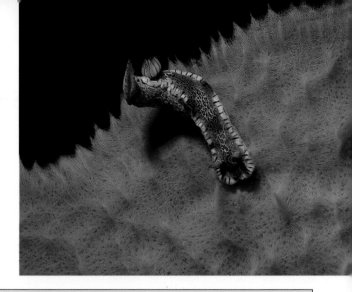

While easily overlooked because of its small size, this ornately designed gold-crowned sea goddess is a member of the order of shell-less snails called nudibranchs.

Keys to Successful Fish Watching

Begin by expanding your underwater *global awareness.* Slow down and look all around you, not just in front of you but turn around, look up, and even behind you. Settle into a relaxed comfortable rate of breathing. Take time to fine tune your buoyancy so that with each inhalation you can feel yourself beginning to rise slightly and as you exhale you slowly sink back down.

Many of the small creatures invite closer observation. While the standard fare of tropical reef fish are easily seen swimming above the coral or sandy bottom, many other kinds of interesting critters prefer to remain hidden under a ledge or blend in so well with their surroundings that swimming fast over the bottom or along the reef doesn't afford enough time for close observation.

Encounters with large marine life are certainly exciting, but these chance encounters don't always happen during each dive. To assure a rewarding dive each time, search for the tiny things, not only the big guys. Explore various habitats that you've overlooked in the past, such as sea grass beds or large areas of sand or rock rubble. You will be amazed to discover all the bizarre creatures and their interesting adaptations for all types of different habitats.

Become better at describing the fish by knowing the difference between a pectoral fin and a ventral fin. And best of all, share each new find with a buddy and use the extra pair of eyes to find even more amazing discoveries. Once you have increased your awareness about the surroundings, listen to your senses. When the sixth sense whispers to you, turn around and look behind you, you might be surprised to see what is watching you. Each dive comes with a blueprint for enjoyment—make the most out of it!

4

Diving in Culebra

Situated in the Vieques Passage, halfway between Puerto Rico and St. Thomas, the island of Culebra is part of a long chain that makes up the geographical boundary of the Caribbean.

Nearly every form of watersports is available throughout Puerto Rico.

One of several charming canalside cafes on Culebra.

Reached by plane from San Juan and Fajardo or by ferry departing from Fajardo, Culebra is an idyllic weekend retreat for Puerto Ricans. The fast pace of San Juan is easily left behind. The definition of traffic here is when the road is shared with one other vehicle. There are no traffic lights, no movie theaters, and no large hotels. Instead, there are modest guest houses and restaurants lining the small canals that transform this charming tropical island into the Venice of Puerto Rico.

For the locals the sea is a way of life. Many people living here commute to work in motorized boats or dinghies. To the few outside visitors the white sand beaches, clear water, and miles of coral reef are the main attraction. The sea surrounds you, and the 20 or more islands and cays that encircle Culebra provide a variety of diving and snorkeling conditions suitable for anyone. The waters around Culebra explode with populations of colorful reef fish like nowhere else in Puerto Rico.

An aerial view of the fringing reefs at the entrance to Hurricane Hole, Culebra.

Amberjack 3

Typical depth range:	50–60 feet
Typical current conditions:	Mild to strong
Expertise required:	Novice
Access:	Boat

Southwest from the marina, in the direction of the many grass-covered rocky islands that decorate the blue waters west of Culebra, the boat stops a short distance offshore. The blue sky over the island of Vieques is seen to the south, and rising up from the sea, to the west, the distant shape of hills and mountains ascend into the morning clouds of the tropical rain forest on the northeast side of Puerto Rico.

Angelfish are common residents of Puerto Rican waters.

Curious about divers and their shining bubbles, jacks often make close passes at divers before departing rapidly.

This hogfish stops at a cleaning station to rid himself of unwanted parasites, which in turn provide a constant food source for the small cleanerfish.

Underwater, schooling silver amberjacks face into the current keeping in tight fighter formation. Out of the profusion of tan-colored soft corals near the bottom, tiny black and yellow striped wrasses set up stations to rid even barracudas of unwanted parasites. A family of large French angels glides among a long line of rocks smothered in delicate sponges and red and black deep-water gorgonians. At the end of the row of rocks is an enormous apartment-sized boulder jutting way up off the flat sand bottom in about 60 feet of water.

Photographers can easily spend the entire dive just circling the rock to find a wealth of subjects and scenes for wide angle or macro. Visibility averages 50-60 feet and currents are mild to strong.

Waves of silver fish called jacks can temporarily fill the water with motion and leave as suddenly as they appeared out of nowhere.

Typical depth range:	20–50 feet
Typical current conditions:	Slight to strong
Expertise:	Intermediate
Access:	Boat

While the name Cayo Raton, meaning Rat Key, may not be exciting, the fish life on this shallow dive will blow you away. One of the 20 or more rocks and islands to the west of Culebra, Cayo Raton is the greatest site to view fish. The boat anchors in a little rock cove on the north side of the cay. There is an underwater plateau that extends 50 or 60 yards out and is flat on top at a depth of 20 to 30 feet. Dropping quickly to 40 or 50 feet,

Displaying her royal crown of blue, the queen angelfish may be the prettiest Caribbean fish of all.

The peacock flounder is born as an upright swimming fish, but as it develops one eye migrates across to join the other eye and the fish lies on its left side, flat on the bottom using one pectoral fin as a dorsal. The fish can change color quickly and glide over the bottom in a wave-like motion.

Often found in pairs, the spotfin butterflyfish is the largest of all butterflyfish in the Caribbean, reaching a maximum of 8 inches.

the reef is buzzing with fish life. Schooling horse-eyed jacks spiral over the reef plateau, speedy bonnetfish zoom in and out of view and brilliant spotfin butterflyfish swim among the lacy pedestals of sea fans where velcro-like yellow and orange armed crinoids are stuffed into many cracks in the reef. Large numbers of magnificent queen angels and parrotfish parade by. Other species include the bizarre peacock flounder that stares up from the sand with a pair of radar round eyes that move independently from each other, and whose mouth appears as if it were placed where it is as an afterthought.

The large concentrations of fish make good wide-angle photo opportunities, while the assortment and abundance of reef fish in general make this a productive fish portrait kind of place. Visibility averages 50 to 75 feet and can easily exceed 100 feet on good days.

Schools of fish thicker than anywhere else in Puerto Rico inhabit the many reefs encircling Culebra.

Tug Boat

Typical depth range:	10–30 feet
Typical current conditions:	Heavy surge when waves are present
Expertise required:	Intermediate
Access:	Boat

On a flat calm day, a tug boat from the West Indian Transport Company ran hard aground atop a small reef miles from the entrance to Hurricane Hole in Culebra. The crew remained on board for days to off-load what they could, then abandoned her. The area surrounding the tug is loaded with small Australian-like reefs that come within striking distance of the surface and for years boaters unfamiliar with the approach to Culebra would follow the sight of this distant tug. A number of boats met the same fate. As a result, the Coast Guard pulled the tug off the reef and sunk her. Years later, Hurricane Hugo moved the tug to where she now rests,

This princess parrotfish belongs in the group of most commonly seen reef fish. Some parrotfish are hermaphroditic and capable of sex reversal.

near her original grounding spot with her bow nestled into the base of one of these shallow reefs.

To the east of Culebra the wreck sits in her shallow grave exposed to seas generated by the steady tradewinds and within sight of the lighthouse on the miniature island of Culebrita. The shallowness of the site means heavy surge on rough days, so it's best dived during calmer weather typical in summer months. The tug boat is impressively intact and corals are beginning to form on the deck and the ship's interior. Easily explored, the wheelhouse is open and relatively diver-friendly. There are hatches and below-deck areas leading to the engine room that are best left to those divers experienced in wreck diving.

There are vast fields of staghorn coral like nowhere else. Steep-walled reefs prove interesting and reveal varieties of territorial damselfish and lots of yellow, black, and white striped sergeant majors, which prefer the better oxygenated shallow water of the reef top.

Photographers are rewarded with classic wreck shots in sunny water with good visibility averaging 60 to 75 feet and ample bottom time for photographing and exploring.

Run aground by its crew, sunk by the Coast Guard, and moved once more by the forces of Hurricane Hugo, this tug boat rests several miles east of the island of Culebra.

5

Diving the Eastern Side of Puerto Rico

Puerto Rico is linked in the east to the Virgin Islands by a broad shallow undersea plateau that rarely dips below 80 feet deep. The many picture-perfect islands scattered about typify one's image of the serene tropics—so well that movie makers have been filming in Puerto Rico for decades.

The cosmopolitan side of Puerto Rico includes the capital city of San Juan with high rise hotel resorts, casinos, and lively nighttime entertainment. The busiest cruise ship port in the Caribbean offers sightseers a look back in time simply by walking through the narrow streets of Old San Juan. Thick-walled Spanish forts with turrets that guarded the city for centuries against pirates, are now protected as a national historical site.

Turning from the Atlantic coastal city of San Juan, southeast toward the Caribbean seashore, the dramatic Luquillo Mountain Range rises nearly 4,000 feet. The cool temperatures inside the misty rain forest of El Yunque turn everything to green. Huge prehistoric-like ferns, canopies of bamboo and roadside waterfalls are being preserved as the U.S. Forest Service's largest tract of tropical forest.

An estimated 100 billion gallons of annual rainfall snakes its way down past villages and towns to the Caribbean Sea. The miles of breezy coconut-palmed beaches are the perfect place for two of the most impressive resorts in the Caribbean. Just about any form of summer recreation including mountain biking, kayaking, parasailing, jet skiing, and, of course, snorkeling, sailing, scuba diving, and the finest golf courses and casinos are available.

In contrast to the enormous resorts, there are modest open-air retreats that also serve up watersports in the Caribbean style.

The 28,000-acre Caribbean National Forest is the only tropical forest in the U.S. National Forest System.

Typical depth:	20–60 feet
Typical current conditions:	Slight to none
Expertise required:	Novice
Access:	Boat

Located offshore from Fajardo are the islands of Palominos and tiny Palomenitos. These two islands are frequented by guests staying at the El Conquistador Resort near Las Croabas. The reef surrounding the deserted island is excellent for snorkeling and diving because its shallow patterned reef is near the shore. The keen diver remains alert because occasional glances out away from the reef, which slopes from 20 feet down to 50 or

The clear warm water and shallow reefs surrounding the tiny eastern island of Palomenitos offers an irresistible invitation to snorkelers and divers.

After extended periods of time underwater searching for and feeding on sponges, jellyfish, and marine plants, green sea turtles rise to the surface to exchange air three or more times before diving again.

Underwater Photography Tips

Before departing for the dive site, have your camera completely set up and check that batteries and flash connections are good by test firing the unit. Bring extra film or cameras and be ready for anything. Store cameras in a safe place away from heavy scuba equipment and out of direct sunlight. If possible, bring fresh water in a small cooler or bucket to soak and clean the camera after diving.

Many of the dive operators understand the special needs of photographers, so take advantage of their knowledge and ask to determine the best lens or subjects before each dive.

Once underwater, search, don't swim. Approach subjects slowly in a non-threatening manner and minimize eye contact. Chasing fish usually yields a greater percentage of uninteresting tail shots. Get as close as possible to your subjects and try to include some blue water in the background by angling upwards. Check, double check, and triple check that controls are set properly, including bracket using distance, F-stops, or flash settings. For more impressive shots, fill the frame corner to corner.

Wide-angle lenses are best suited for reef scenes, diver portraits or silhouettes, caves, tunnels, and shipwrecks. Fish portraits are more easily captured using longer lenses such as a 105mm or a 60mm on cameras in housings, while the 28mm or 35mm lenses work well with the Nikonos.

Close-up and macro is ideal for night dives and generally produces sharp, colorful images when visibility is poor. Avoid trying to capture small fish with this set-up because the framers tend to scare them away.

Pictures of divers man-handling marine life are quickly becoming a thing of the past. Please remember, no photo is worth harming even the tiniest marine organism.

Learn to shoot. Shoot to learn.

---

60 feet, reveals giant eagle rays that glide by silently leaving behind no trail. Hawksbill turtles can be observed resting on the bottom among a tangle of soft coral.

Out in the sand within sight of the fringing reef, the eyes of southern rays buried under the camouflage of sand can be detected. Adorning the reef face are numerous common sea fans, sea whips, and sea plumes standing 2 to 4 feet off the bottom. This dive is an easy walk in the park and good for many frames to the underwater photographer.

Yellowhead jawfish inhabit sandy areas and hover vertically above burrows excavated out of sand and coral rubble. They not only use their mouths for digging, but the males also incubate eggs in their mouths.

Rising out of the sand, this tough-skinned southern stingray dumps sand from his back, but doesn't rid himself of the pesty remora. Eagle rays and mantas can leap clear out of the water, perhaps in an attempt to free themselves of such unwanted guests.

Typical depth range:	20–50 feet
Typical current conditions:	Slight to moderate
Expertise required:	Novice
Access:	Boat from San Juan or Fajardo

At Diablo, one of the small low-lying islands in a chain stretching away from the lighthouse at Cabezas De San Juan, the reef has the appearance of a well-manicured coral garden. Divers are likely to encounter other dive boats as this prized site is the favorite of local dive clubs and operators. Great barracudas curiously observe divers. Large formations of yellow and white goatfish and neon blue chromis stay near the predominantly hard coral reef.

A most unusual encounter was a lone West Indian manatee that had wandered miles out to sea from its usual coastal mangrove habitat. The sea cow, as they are commonly called, was easy to approach, slow-moving, and seemed to enjoy having its back scratched by divers who were very willing to comply.

Octocorallian polyps have eight tentacles or feather-like pinnules that filter the water for nutrients and attach themselves to the bottom or substrate using a single holdfast.

The garden-like appearance of reefs near Fajardo have long been favorite spots for local dive clubs.

Typical depth range:	3–30 feet
Typical current conditions:	Mild to moderate
Expertise required:	Novice
Access:	Boat

One of the northernmost small cays on the east side of Puerto Rico is simply called Lobos and averages in depth from just below the surface down to 30 feet. This area is loaded with caves, tunnels, and archways that make an excellent second or third dive of the day. There are enormous rounded mounds of boulder star coral that dwarf divers in comparison. Many smaller leaf, plate, and sheet coral make up the porous outlines of the reef, and on patrol for good grazing grounds are tightly packed schools of blue tangs swimming through brilliant shafts of sunlight radiating from the surface. Small sharp-nosed pufferfish turn on a dime while doing their impression of an undersea hummingbird.

Blue tangs frequently school with other surgeonfish and doctorfish and will descend, head down in unison to graze on algae.

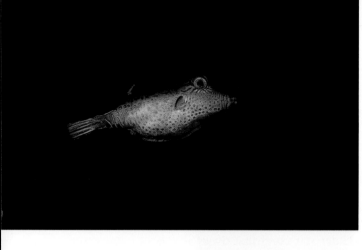

Smallest of the puffers, 2–3 inches, the sharpnose puffer moves about underwater much like a helicopter can maneuver in air.

At night arrowhead crabs are among the many crustaceans that can be seen foraging for food. Daylight hours you'll find these spider-like crabs tucked into hiding spots along the base of the reef.

At night the act and characters change to include some zany crustaceans, eels searching for meals, and corals that flower with jelly-like polyps that serve to trap squiggly worms that explode on contact after being attracted by underwater lights.

When peering beneath just about any ledge, you will be stared right back at by dozens of pairs of reflective eyes that belong to red night shrimp or peppermint shrimp. By daybreak the nocturnal creatures head for the darkest recesses in the reef and parrotfish swim free of their nightly mucous cocoons to once again take up flight as the sand-producing crop dusters of the Caribbean. According to Dr. Bill Alevizon, author of *Caribbean Coral Reef Ecology* (Pisces Books, Houston, Texas), an adult parrotfish defecates almost a ton of "sand" each year. So, the next time you're walking along a beautiful, pristine Caribbean beach, you might consider the fact that much of what you're walking on is fish "poop."

Typical depth range:	60–90 feet
Typical current conditions:	Mild to none (surface can be rough)
Expertise required:	Intermediate
Access:	Boat from Palmas Del Mar

Approximately five miles out to sea from the Palmas Del Mar Resort near Humacao lies an undisturbed tract of reef named "The Reserve." The diving out from the resort begins to change from the shallow reefs of the east to the deep reefs and walls of the south and southwest. The visibility is exceptionally clear, 75 to 100 feet, but the boat ride out to this site can be rough. Divers prone to seasickness should take precautions.

Shy and difficult to photograph, queen triggerfish are remarkable due to their various shades of purple, blue, turquoise, and green.

With black and yellow colorings that distinguish French angelfish from grey angelfish, juveniles of the two species each appear black with bright yellow vertical lines and can be told apart only by the presence of a yellow circled tail of the French, versus a yellow band on the tail of a grey.

Once underwater, the dark shapes of the reef are taken in, rising up from the light blue-colored sand. The tops of these rounded hills of coral are in 60 to 70 feet of water. The sand channels that all point farther out to sea are in 80 to 90 feet. Diving computers are provided for customers not carrying their own.

The surrounding reefs are clean, and excellent photographic opportunities exist to catch grey angelfish nipping at the divers' bubbles. This unusual behavior makes it easy to get in real close for some exciting shots. The concentrations of invertebrates and small reef fish are quite impressive. The occurrence of large bright clumps of orange elephant ear sponges and other odd-shaped sponges paint the bottom in a wild assembly of colors. The sight of a school of silver and black Atlantic spadefish lends itself to the feeling of being in a large fish tank.

Atlantic spadefish usually inhabit open water in small schools, occasionally forming huge schools with individuals reaching a maximum of 3 feet.

Grey angelfish swim gracefully about the reef, usually in pairs, biting off bits of tasty sponges.

Purple and gold fairy basslets orient their belly to the ceiling and swim upside down, favoring the darkened areas created by overhangs, ledges, or caves. ▶

Typical depth range:	50–70 feet
Typical current conditions:	Mild, some surge
Expertise required:	Novice
Access:	Boat

This popular spot is only five or ten minutes out of the marina at Palmas Del Mar. The main difference between the farther offshore sights and The Cracks is that the visibility is normally not as good—in the 40 to 60 feet range. The topography is what attracts divers. The ancient base of this inshore reef has been eroding away creating underwater trenches and large ledges with overhangs that come together to form tunnels and arches. Most of the time divers can only be detected from above by bubbles percolating up through the porous coral. Do not be mistaken, however, this is not a cave dive. There are only a few places that provide overhead.

For photographers using flash and wide-angle lenses, debris loosened by exhaled bubbles and careless fins can cause unwanted backscatter, so the first pass is generally more productive for clear pictures or switch to close-up or macro.

The sides of these ledges are loaded with dazzling purple and orange fairy basslets and black barred soldierfish. Back on top of this stringy maze numerous reef fish abound to keep your shutter finger happy.

Like molten lava flowing out from underneath the coral, orange elephant ear sponges can grow in a variety of irregular shapes and thrive at depths to 130 feet or more.

Typical depth range:	50–70 feet
Typical current conditions:	Mild, if any
Expertise required:	Intermediate
Access:	Boat

This site was named after Dr. Seuss's storybook town in "How the Grinch Stole Christmas." There is a large teardrop-shaped coral rise at the center of an incredible underwater amphitheater of coral formations that come out of the sand at a depth of 70 feet to form bunches of mini walls that ascend to 50 feet or so. The undersides of these walls are crowded with orange cup corals, red rope sponges, and orange ball sponges. The small holes in the reef are full of fairy basslets. The yellow, brown, and white longsnout butterflyfish flits about here and this is also a choice location for seeing southern stingrays and great barracudas. The edge of the reef facing the slight current is bustling with blue and brown chromis. The

Not all the deep diving is done on walls. There are impressive spur and grove formations as well as fringing reefs.

sunny reef tops are packed with tan soft corals and lavender sea fans. French and grey angelfish and even tiger and Nassau grouper add to the fish life.

This dive site is located 5 or 6 miles east of Palmas Del Mar in the direction of Vieques, so the visibility is unbelievably clear at 100 feet. Because it is in open ocean, the surface can at times be somewhat rough.

The smallest and more secretive of the Caribbean butterflyfish, the long snout butterflyfish uses its long pointed snout to root up small marine invertebrates.

Typical depth range:	45–60 feet
Typical current conditions:	Mild
Expertise required:	Novice
Access:	Boat

   This dive site is situated closer to shore than Whoville, but shares that same clarity of water. The creatures usually associated with night dives, such as reef squid, octopus, and lobsters are out and about during daylight hours as well. In fact, not only can one see the octopus itself, but evidence

The common Caribbean reef squid relies on camouflage, powerful water jets, and ink to evade predators; squid are readily accepted in the dietary plans of most undersea carnivores.

Flamingo tongue snails use their disguise of a giraffe-like spotted skin covering the shell to blend in with the gorgonians that they feed on.

such as a pile of neatly cleaned shells in front of an ideally sized hole, gives a clue that an octopus has been feeding there recently. With excellent night vision, as well as other alert senses, the octopus leaves its den each night and locates food in the form of shellfish nearby, returning quickly to devour the meal and toss out the "dirty dish" afterwards. These masters of camouflage and supreme contortionists must be cautious because almost every undersea creature enjoys the taste of octopus.

A line of colorful coral ledges and some foxhole swim-throughs create long shaded areas spinning with goatfish, squirrelfish, and the unusual dark-colored black and white high hat. The reef area is easily navigated, and reveals a bounty of strange creatures such as the thumbnail-size flamingo tongue snails that cling to the base of the yellow, green, and purple sea fans.

6

Diving in La Parguera
(The Grand Savannah)

In contrast to the lush tropical vegetation of the northeast, the southwest has vast dry savannahs of yellow grass with green rolling hills dotted with shade trees resembling those found in Africa. All the natural features here combine to resemble the plains of the Serengeti.

Only hours before the diving begins at La Parguera, nature paints the sky a glorious color of red.

The Paradores

A network of lodging fashioned after the Paradores of Spain. The inns are established throughout Puerto Rico near historical places such as San German, Puerto Rico's second oldest city, or on the grounds of old coffee plantations, high in the mountains. Most of these country-style inns are close to areas of natural interest like the Karst limestone region, which is loaded with caves and a thermal spring; the world famous surfing and sunning beaches along the west coast; or other seaside communities blessed with natural wonders such as La Parguera, along the south coast, best known for its phosphorescent bay. Several sites include the panoramic cliffs along the north shore, El Yunque rain forest, and the east coast of Puerto Rico so popular with the watersports enthusiast.

This system of affordably priced hotels began during the 1970s under the direction of the Puerto Rico Tourism Company. Each of the eighteen paradores differs not only in the variety of settings but also in atmosphere and facilities ranging from guest houses in rural surroundings to hotels near golf courses and airports. All paradores share the same good service and family atmosphere. For more information contact the Puerto Rico Tourism Company (800) 721-2400.

The shoreline around Guanica and La Parguera is made up of mangrove lagoons and sandy beaches. The small fishing village of La Parguera fills with visitors on weekends and holidays, plying the calm lagoon waterways. The endless canals are lined with colorfully painted houseboats and homes built on stilts. The seemingly floating islands of mangrove trees provide a unique ecology and nursery for all types of reef fishes.

Here is a bay with heavy concentrations of microscopic organisms known to the scientific community as dinoflagellates, but more commonly known as bioluminescence. The eerie glow of phosphorescence attracts many nighttime visitors to see the natural nighttime light show.

For divers the name La Parguera is synonymous with wall diving. Each ocean is said to have its own signature blend of blue and it's this clear electric blue of the deep Caribbean that excites divers of all levels.

Stretching over 20 miles east and west from Guanica to well past La Parguera, there is a tumultuous drop-off of continental proportion that would resemble the rim of the Grand Canyon. The first drop begins at an average of 65 feet and falls away steeply to a broad shelf at a depth of 600 feet. From here it continues well beyond two miles deep to join the oceanic depths of the Venezuelan Basin.

The impressive scale of a drop such as this can be overwhelming. Divers explore only the top of the wall between 60 and 130 feet. The rest remains a secret temptation known only to the creatures that inhabit the purple-indigo world beyond.

In the small fishing village of La Parguera, best known for its phosphorescent bay, traditional wooden boats are rented for exploring the inner mangrove lagoon.

Black Wall drops vertically beginning at around 70 feet. This is only a tiny section of a wall that stretches more than 20 miles from Guanica toward Cabo Rojo along the southwest coast of Puerto Rico. ▶

Typical depth range:	60–130 feet
Typical current conditions:	Light to moderate
	Surface conditions can be rough,
	3 to 5 feet
Expertise required:	Intermediate
Access:	Boat

The boat departs from Paraguera and travels east on the peaceful water of the inner lagoon, then south through a cut in the low lying islands and barrier reef to an area referred to as "Black Wall."

Scooped out of the top of the wall is a large three-sided bowl that drops to hundreds of feet below. Along the top and sides and extending down to 165

feet are enormous red and black deep-water gorgonians mixed with bushy trees of black coral. This is one of the steepest drop-offs along the wall.

These waters are home to the baboon-faced black durgon that occupies deep-water sites. These triggerfish swim in midwater or just below the surface. Along the leading edge of the reef, large dog snappers, bright blue

This Spanish hogfish is caught going over the wall where deep-water sea fans commonly grow at depths greater than 60 feet.

At certain times of the year sponges like this purple tube sponge release a steady stream of reproductive spores that resembles smoke rising from underwater smoke stacks.

queen angels, and Spanish hogfish zoom in and out of settings of orange and red coral, lavender rope sponges, and yellow and purple tube sponges.

The wall is alive in a pleasing array of colors. Underwater photographers would find little reason for leaving the spot carved out of the wall. The rich, warm colors contrast nicely against the clear deep-blue background.

Typical depth range:	60–70 feet
Typical current conditions:	Little to none
Expertise required:	Novice
Access:	Boat

As the name implies, barracudas are very commonplace here, keeping a watchful eye over their watery domain. This site is inland from the Black Wall at a depth of 70 feet. There are fingers of sand separating large spur and groove coral formations. Strong stands of elkhorn coral reach up

towards the sunlight. Surrounding the mighty elkhorn coral are more delicate assemblages of staghorn coral making it essential to maintain good buoyancy control to avoid damaging the immaculate coral arrangements.

Here also black durgons are abundant, and rock beauties can be observed snacking on nests of sergeant major eggs. Lavender sea fans sway back and forth, and out in the sand, piles of coral debris give residence to long, eel-like tilefish. Tiny bluish chalk bass hover in small groups over sand bottoms near coral debris and can be approached and photographed using slow non-threatening advances.

The head of a heavy-bodied green moray may be seen poking out of recesses along the side of the reef, and close watch reveals antennae of heavily-armored spiny lobsters.

◄ *Black durgon are triggerfish that prefer deep open-water areas. They are equipped with a fin on top of their head, just above the eye, which can be raised to lock themselves inside cracks or crevices for protection.*

Southern sennets are in the barracuda family, but only reach 18 inches in length. They form slow moving schools that sometimes break to make circles.

Typical depth range:	65–100 feet
Typical current conditions:	Slight to moderate
Expertise required:	Intermediate
Access:	Boat

Several miles southeast from La Parguera and within sight of the dry forest hills of Guanica is "The Buoy," named after a buoy that marked this site for scientific purposes. All that remains now is a large cement block and some of the healthiest coral and invertebrates stretching out in all directions. The entire area is remarkably intact and shows little, if any, signs of damage.

Many of the reefs around Puerto Rico have remained virtually intact and unexplored for centuries. Even today most of the diving is done from small boats with no other boats in sight. ▶

◀ *A diver witnesses a hungry rock beauty feasting on a purple nest of sergeant major eggs. The much distressed protector of the nest waits nearby, unable to defend the nest against the sheer size and determination of the attacker.*

Divers capture the many wonders of the ocean environment near La Parguera and return with personalized videotapes to share with family and friends.

The drop-off is not as sheer as other spots and slopes down from 65 feet at steeper than a 45° angle. While depths in excess of 100 feet are easily reached, 80 feet is a good average, allowing plenty of time for exploring. Narrow canyons carved deeply into the reef face, all leading to the wall and forming rivers of sand, cascade well out of sight.

Abundant on the deep sloping reef are giant red-brown barrel sponges large enough to hide the diver. Pink vase sponges crawling with brittlestars and azure vase sponges hold their color well even at 100 feet. Twenty-armed golden crinoids belonging to the feather star class can be seen hiding their velcro sticky arms.

Divers in the company of a wealth of reef fishes find it easy to cruise four or five of the hard coral canyons before returning beneath the boat.

◄ *The healthy condition of many of Puerto Rico's offshore reefs is reflected in all the colors of the spectrum in even the smallest area.*

Typical depth range:	55–70 feet
Typical current conditions:	Slight to none
Expertise required:	Novice
Access:	Boat

Out of a flat sand bottom from a depth of 70 feet, rise long rounded hills of mound and boulder corals splashed with brilliant orange, yellow, and red rope pore sponges, and large colonies of sea plumes and fans.

Schools of little electric blue chromis swim in midwater above the reefs and nearly a dozen varieties of wrasses swim dizzily round the seascape. Large French angelfish that feed on sponges have adopted the curious habit of following divers while playfully nipping at the steady supply of bubbles released on their way to the surface. A large sandy area in the center of all this coral is a proven site to spy southern stingrays concealed under or swimming over the sand.

Rock beauties rarely stray more than 12 inches away from the numerous ins and outs provided by the coral reef.

Typical depth range:	65–100 feet
Typical current conditions:	Mild to none
Expertise required:	Intermediate
Access:	Boat

Situated approximately 7 miles south of Parguera, named for an extraordinary shark encounter, the reef is carpeted with artistically displayed corals and sponges, making this spot very visually exciting.

Small narrow canyons wind their way to the wall and the visibility averages around 75 feet with frequent days in excess of 100 feet. The clear water makes it easy to catch a glimpse of the fast moving pelagics such as cero mackerel or widespread schools of grey ocean triggerfish.

The reef itself is budding with creatures like purple-tipped sea anemones with their resident Pederson shrimp. Clusters of smooth brown tube sponges occasionally form shapes like moose antlers. Tangled masses of pink and red rope sponges, often covered with winding chains of golden zooanthids, add lovely combinations of color. Tightly packed corals are found above 100 feet.

Typical of any section along the 20 miles of wall that hosts a wide diversity of tropical fish, divers may see an endless stream of dark purple and orange creole wrasses winging the water with their pectoral fins.

Often seen in open water along the edges of drop-offs, creole wrasse swim constantly during the day using their pectoral fins and form long streaming schools.

Typical depth range:	55–75 feet
Typical current conditions:	Mild to none
Expertise required:	Novice
Access:	Boat

In from the wall towards shore, still several miles out to sea, sits an airplane motor with the propeller lying alone in the sand. The whereabouts of the rest of the aircraft remains a mystery.

Miles from any airport, this airplane motor sits alone on the seafloor. The whereabouts of the rest of the aircraft remains a mystery.

Because of their size and ability to change color to blend in with the environment, many blennies, like this diamond blenny, are easily overlooked.

Fortunately for divers, there is an area not far from where the motor rests, where the reefs are shaped to form underwater amphitheaters. The sides of the reef are honeycombed with deep holes and cracks providing divers with a chance to see spotted moray eels, porkfish, and schools of yellow and silver striped French grunts.

There is a location where two overhangs merge to form a box canyon. A hollow at the back of this canyon is wildly sprayed with encrusting sponges in every shade of red. Squirrelfish and blackbarred soldierfish prefer to linger here shaded from the sunlight radiating down through the opening. This setting proves to be irresistible for photographers.

67

Diving the West Coast—
Desecheo Island

The western end of Puerto Rico runs in an almost straight line north to south for 35 miles. The two cities, Mayaguez and Aguadilla, have major airports that can accommodate large jets as well as direct flights from the United States.

The two smaller communities of Boqueron and Rincón best exemplify life along the west coast. If you like coconut palms or what they represent, you'll love it here. The tranquil bays of sparkling clear water and white sand beaches offer a perfect place to hang your hammock from palm trees that grow out over the water.

Puerto Rico's west coast, blessed with calm seas and gentle breezes near shore, also offers high voltage diving adventure in the form of two offshore islands named Mona and Desecheo.

Surfers evaluate conditions and pray for typical winter storms to bring big surf to Puerto Rico's surfing capital of Rincón.

The placid waters of Boqueron Bay on Puerto Rico's west side offer ideal settings for picnics and beach outings.

Fifty miles west of Mayaguez is rugged Mona Island. Situated in between Puerto Rico and the Dominican Republic in the rough waters of the Mona Passage, Mona is said to be the Galapagos of the Caribbean. The island is maintained as a nature refuge and permits must be obtained from the Department of Natural and Environmental Resources before visits can be made. Dive operators plan special trips there, usually once a month on weekends, to take dedicated nature lovers to see 200-foot cliffs riddled with caves, yard-long iguanas, colonies of sea birds, and colorful tropical fish.

This remote island is surrounded by big seas and clear water and has no facilities. Diving and camping trips to Mona require advance planning, expert seamanship, and a true appreciation for roughing it.

Another adventure is Desecheo, very possibly the best small island in the Caribbean for wonderfully unspoiled diving. The island is 15 miles west of the surfing community of Rincón and can easily be reached by boats that hold 6 passengers. The trip can be made in 35 to 40 minutes. Desecheo fully deserves a "five-star rating" as one of the Caribbean's best dive sites.

Typical depth range: 60–80 feet
Typical current conditions: Light to strong
Expertise required: Novice
Access: Boat

Reported as the second deepest place in the entire ocean, the Puerto Rican Trench is located just north of Puerto Rico and spans more than 500 miles from east to west. There is a submarine canyon that comes up from nearly 30,000 feet and situated at the top of this canyon is the uninhabit-

Enormous sea fans, clear water, and mountains of healthy coral easily make Desecheo Island one of the best small islands for diving in the entire Caribbean.

Sea bass, like this coney, generally perch themselves upon conspicuous places and have been identified in three different color phases. The brown phase, the red and white bi-color phase, and the seldom-seen yellow or golden phase. All phases share the distinct blue spots.

ed island of Desecheo. This detail alone accounts for the overwhelming variety and abundance of colorful marine organisms that crowd every available spot on the rocks and reef that surround the island.

While there are numerous excellent dives around Desecheo, the back side away from Puerto Rico is preferred by many divers for its calm surface conditions.

The most impressive aspect of the reef is the extra-healthy appearance of the castle-shaped boulder corals, as well as six-foot sea fans, colonies of flower coral, endless sprawling sheet and lettuce coral, and fantastically colorful sponges.

Dense schools of yellow and white goatfish, pairs of reef butterflyfish and rock beauties are here in every phase of development. Several uncommon fish species can be observed, such as the web burrfish and coneys in the golden phase. There are many indescribable colors and shapes integrated with the flourishing corals that make this a must-see experience.

Typical depth range:	25–100+ feet
Typical current conditions:	Moderate to strong
Expertise required:	Intermediate
Access:	Boat

The classical myth of Poseidon (Neptune in Roman mythology), the king of the ocean, and his beautiful wife Amphitrite, has them living beneath the sea in a golden palace.

There is a place like this that stands alone to the north of Desecheo and closest to the colossal depths of the ocean trench. It is here that a mighty mountain of rock juts up from the surrounding seafloor and in a supernatural way is decorated with a profusion of yellow, orange, and golden sponges that justifies this area being named Yellow Reef.

Displaying a false eye-spot thought to confuse predators, pairs of foureye butterflyfish flutter about the reef tops. Of the five varieties of butterflyfish found in the Caribbean, the foureye butterflyfish is the most common.

Redlip blennys vary in color from reddish brown to grey. They are extremely territorial and prefer to perch upon their pectoral fins in shallow rocky reef areas.

Not only the colors and shapes but also the many different textures of coral and sponges create a sensory extravaganza for divers visiting Puerto Rico.

Brilliant powder blue sargassum triggerfish are very shy and normally prefer outer reef and offshore banks deeper than 80 feet.

The golden glow from the surface reveals a straight line of dark blue water where the face of this sculpted rock wall drops unhesitatingly vertical, beginning with a sharp undercut. Current-driven nutrients bathe the magnificent seascape, giving such rich diversity to marine organisms glued to the reef that one simply cannot find an area not dripping with color. For photographers, one dive or one roll of film just is not sufficient.

The dive begins at 30 feet where the flat wall leads down to 60 or 70 feet. There the rock reef shelves and splits in all directions forming large caves at 90 to 100 feet.

Yellow Reef has many other wonders, from tiny spinyhead blennys that stick their heads out of small wormholes darting out and back in a lightning quick pace to grab suspended particles of food, to humpback whales on their seasonal migrations north (January–March). The sizeable fish population includes tiger grouper, princess parrotfish, sargassum triggerfish, and the animated red-lipped blenny.

Even the most seasoned divers have reacted to this dive as being the best dive ever!

Typical depth range:	10–80 feet
Typical current conditions:	Mild to strong
Expertise required:	Intermediate
Access:	Boat

Around the northwest point of Desecheo, there is a peninsula of large rocks that form a barrier from the open ocean swells to the north. Inside this cover, the shoreline is riddled with rock caves and a crescent-shaped pebble beach.

You can begin the dive out from shore in water 60 to 80 feet deep and end up by swimming in towards the rocky shoreline. The steep walled stone canyons near shore are predominantly one color, red. The colonies of corallites are overgrown with sponges, algae, and other encrusting organisms that prefer the shallow canyon walls and cave ceilings. The colors are incredible red-orange and purple, and there are a great deal of choice spots for nurse sharks to rest in. The ocean is very bountiful in this area.

The boat ride to this site revealed a pod of spinner dolphins leaping and tumbling clear of the water.

Venus sea fans can grow just under the surface and are usually shallower than 35 feet, but throughout Puerto Rico they are found deeper than 100 feet.

Least common throughout the Caribbean and simply called reef butterflyfish, these fish pose a challenge to underwater photographers unwilling to wait quietly near their course of travel.

▲ *Playful spinner dolphins are easily the highlight of any boat trip from Rincón to the legendary island of Desecheo. They are named after their ability to leap clear of the water and perform barrel rolls and flips end over end.*

The abundance and variety of hard corals provide an excellent habitat for tropical fish and creatures. ▶

Candlesticks

Typical depth range: 60–90 feet
Typical current conditions: Mild to moderate
Expertise required: Intermediate
Access: Boat

This dive is good from the bottom up. The unbelievable blue, reflected back from the sand channels, and the clarity of the water allow one to make out the forms and textures of the coral 80 feet below. The dominant coral is boulder coral in the shape of thick piles of melted wax, the undersides of which are laced with bright yellow-orange icing sponges. This, together with the bramble of rope pour sponges, stony flower corals, and assorted exotic reef fish, creates a visual cornucopia of brilliant marine life.

Crossing the fifteen miles of open sea to return to Rincón, expect the unexpected. Encounters with pilot whales, humpback whales and playful spinner dolphins will send people running for their cameras.

Humpback Whales

During part of an annual migration, groups of humpback whales can be sighted in the waters surrounding Puerto Rico from January through March. Equally exciting as seeing the whales are the sounds and songs that can be heard underwater from miles away. These same whales are observed by throngs of whale watchers each summer off the New England coast where they return each year to feed on krill.

Whales breed in precise relation to the amount of food in the water. If food is plentiful, the whales return to the warmer tropical water and breed. Courtship depends upon the individual's ability to outperform his rival with the most absorbing song and the wildest body movements including spy-hopping, lob-tailing, tail slapping, and breaching. Once a partner has been agreed upon, the pair embraces belly to belly, face to face, and stroking each other with their pectoral fins, they accelerate in unison for the surface. The two break the surface together and fall away from each other in a tremendous splash.

The gestation period is just under a year, so the next season the family returns to the warmer water to give birth. The bull and cow are usually escorted by another adult female to assist in the birthing.

Sometime after the newborn calf is lifted to the surface for its first breath, the mother will begin feeding her young the equivalent of 800 glasses of milk each day. The family will stay around warm water long enough to get the newborn strong and capable of the long journey ahead. For months the parents eat next to nothing until they, as a family, enter into the nutrient-rich water of the North Atlantic. Should something untimely happen to the calf during the trip, the mother will continue to support her young upon her back until it disintegrates.

◄ *Good water quality and few unnatural disturbances provide an ideal environment for corals and sponges to flourish.*

8

Safe, Smart Diving

By far, injuries occurring to divers are usually a direct result of action taken or not taken. Avoid the most common problems affecting air spaces in the ear and mask by equalizing early and often, and don't continue to descend if any discomfort occurs.

At the conclusion of each dive, save enough precious air in the tank for at least a three-minute safety decompression stop at around 15 feet. Maintain proper buoyancy and remain well enough away from the reef to avoid unnecessary burns from stinging coral or abrasions from a direct hit. When swimming into tight spaces, be sure to make room for your tank by bringing the front of your body closest to that which you can see.

By increasing your global awareness and learning to dive well, you will increase your safe enjoyment of a form of recreation unlike any other on earth.

Preparation

Before you leave home, make sure all of your dive gear is in good working order and that all items that must be serviced yearly—especially regulators—have been. There is nothing as aggravating as getting on the boat, arriving on your first dive site, only to discover that your octopus is free-flowing. If you wear a mask with a prescription or have trouble finding a mask that fits you correctly, bring a backup mask. Masks have been known to arrive at a different destination than you, fall overboard, or break. You won't be comfortable with a borrowed mask if you can't see or if it keeps leaking. Finally, if you haven't been diving for six months or more, especially if you have logged fewer than 20 dives, it might be a good idea to take a practice or refresher dive either in a local pool at home or with an instructor at a dive store in the islands before you head for deep water.

◀ The creole wrasse is another common resident of the reefs surrounding Puerto Rico.

Reef Etiquette and Bouyancy Control

While moorings may go a long way toward reducing anchor damage to our reefs, so far there is nothing to protect them from damage by divers . . . except divers. Dive sites tend to be located where the reefs and walls display the most beautiful corals and sponges. And it only takes a moment— an inadvertently placed hand or knee on the coral or an unaware brush or kick with a fin—to destroy this fragile living part of our delicate ecosystem. Only a moment can make a dive site a little less spectacular spot for other divers. Luckily, it only takes a little extra preparation and consideration to preserve it for generations of divers to come.

So if you're a new diver, a little rusty after a long hiatus on dry land, diving with new equipment, or if you just need a little reminder, here are a few helpful tips for protecting reefs:

1. Maintain proper buoyancy control and avoid over-weighting.
2. Use correct weight belt position to stay horizontal, i.e., raise the belt above your waist to elevate your feet/fins, and move it lower toward your hips to lower them.
3. Use your tank position in the backpack as a balance weight, i.e., raise your backpack on the tank to lower your legs, and lower the backpack on the tank to raise your legs.
4. Watch for buoyancy changes during a dive trip. During the first couple of days, you'll probably breathe a little harder and need a bit more weight than the last few days.
5. Be careful about buoyancy loss at depth; the deeper you go the more your wet suit compresses, and the more buoyancy you lose.
6. Photographers must be extra careful. Cameras and equipment affect buoyancy. Changing f-stops, framing a subject, and maintaining position for a photo often conspire to prohibit the ideal "no-touch" approach on a reef. So, when you must use "holdfasts," choose them intelligently.
7. Avoid full leg kicks when working close to the bottom and when leaving a photo scene. When you inadvertently kick something, stop kicking! Seems obvious, but some divers either semi-panic or are totally oblivious when they bump something.
8. When swimming in strong currents, be extra careful about leg kicks and handholds.
9. Attach dangling gauges, computer consoles, and octopus regulators. They are like miniature wrecking balls to a reef.
10. Never drop boat anchors onto a reef.

Considered to be the redwoods of the Caribbean, elkhorn coral prefers shallow fringing reef areas.

Hazardous Marine Life

Diving around Puerto Rico isn't really hazardous. It's divers who are hazardous. When was the last time a stand of fire coral pursued a diver to sting him? Most stings, scrapes, and punctures are due to divers inadvertently bumping into coral or touching a creature that instinctively defends itself against its giant aggressor. Some injuries are harmless and merely uncomfortable. Others may require medical attention. Ideally, we shouldn't touch anything underwater, but it does happen and it does hurt!

Watch out for the following:

Fire Coral. Mustard brown in color, fire coral is most often found in shallower waters encrusting dead gorgonians or coral. Contact causes a burning sensation that lasts for several minutes and sometimes causes red welts on the skin. If you rub against fire coral, do not try to rub the affected area as you will spread the small stinging particles. Upon resurfacing, apply meat tenderizer to relieve the sting and then antibiotic cream. Cortisone cream can also reduce any inflammation.

Sponges. They may be beautiful but sponges can also pack a powerful punch with fine spicules that sting on contact. While bright reddish-brown ones are often the stinging kind, familiarly called dread red, they are not the only culprits. If you touch a stinging sponge, scrape the area with the edge of your dive knife. Home remedies include mild vinegar or ammonia solutions to ease the pain, but most of it will subside within a day. Again, cortisone cream might help.

Sea Urchins. The urchin's most dangerous weapon is its spines, which can penetrate neoprene wetsuits, booties, and gloves with ease. You'll know you've been jabbed from the instant pain. Urchins tend to be more common in shallow areas near shore and come out of their shelters under coral heads at night. If you are beach diving, beware of urchins that may be lying on the shallow reef you have to cross to reach deeper water. Don't move across it on your hands and knees and start swimming as soon as possible. Injuries should be attended to as soon as possible because infection can occur. Minor punctures require removal of the spine and treatment with an antibiotic cream. More serious ones should be looked at by a doctor.

Bristle Worms. Bristle worms make a great subject for macro photography, but don't touch them to move them to the perfect spot. Use a strobe arm or dive knife. Contact will result in tiny stinging bristles being embedded in the skin and resulting in a burning feeling or welt. You can try to scrape the bristles off with the edge of a dive knife. Otherwise, they will work themselves out within a few days. Again, cortisone cream can help minimize any inflammation.

Sea Wasps. A potentially serious diving hazard, sea wasps are small, potent jellyfish with four stinging tentacles, and they generally swim within a few feet of the surface at night. If sea wasps have been spotted in the water where you are planning to do a night dive, take caution. Don't linger on the surface upon entry into the water. When you return, turn your dive light off as it attracts them and exit the water as quickly as possible. Their sting is very painful and leaves a red welt as a reminder. Do NOT try to push them away from your area of ascent by sending air bubbles to the surface from your regulator. The bubbles may break off their tentacles and you won't be able to see where the stinging tentacles are. If you are allergic to bee stings and sea wasps have been spotted at the dive site, consider foregoing the dive as you will most likely have the same reaction to a sea wasp sting.

Scorpionfish. They may be one of the sea's best camouflaged creatures, but if you receive a puncture by the poisonous spines that are hidden among its fins, you'll know you've found a scorpionfish. They tend to lie on the bottom or on coral, so, unless you are lying on the bottom or on the reef—which you shouldn't be (see "Reef Etiquette and Buoyancy Control")—they shouldn't present a problem. Should you get stung, go to a hospital or a doctor as soon as possible because the sting can result in severe allergic reactions, and pain and infection are almost guaranteed.

Stingrays. These creatures are harmless unless you sit or step on them. If you harass them, you may discover the long, barbed stinger located at the base of the tail which can cause a very painful wound that can be deep and become infected. If you suffer from a sting, go to a hospital or seek a doctor's care immediately. But the best policy is to leave them alone, and they'll leave you alone in return.

Eels. Similarly, eels won't bother you unless you bother them. It is best not to hand feed them, especially when you don't know if other eels or hazardous fish such as barracudas or sharks are in the area. And don't put your hand in a dark hole because it might just house an eel. Eels have extremely poor eyesight and cannot always distinguish between food and your hand. If you are bitten by an eel, don't try to pull your hand away— their teeth are extraordinarily sharp. Let the eel release it and then surface (at the required slow rate of ascent), apply first aid, and then head for the nearest hospital.

Sharks. Although not an extremely common sight for divers, when sharks do appear, it is a cause for celebration and fascination. As a rule, most of the sharks you will encounter are not aggressive and will not attack divers. However, it is wise not to feed them or harass them. If you are unlucky enough to be mistaken for a meal, the nearest hospital is the most logical next stop.

Barracuda. Barracudas have a miserable reputation. In fact, they are somewhat shy although unnervingly curious. They will hover near enough to divers to observe what they are so interested in, but just try to photograph them and they keep their distance. You'll see them on almost every dive. Don't bother them—and they won't bother you.

Diving Accidents

Diving is a safe sport and there are very few accidents compared to the number of divers and dives made each year. However, occasionally accidents do occur, and emergency medical treatment should be sought immediately. If you are diving with a local dive operation, they will be equipped to handle any situation expediently. If a diving injury or decompression sickness occurs when you are on your own, here are some important emergency numbers to contact:

Emergency 911. The police department is equipped to handle all emergencies or access to any additional services that may be required, including Coast Guard helicopters, hospitals, police and fire department dive teams, and recompression chambers.

Divers Alert Network/DAN. This is a nonprofit membership association of individuals and organizations sharing a common interest in diving safety. It assists in the treatment of underwater diving accidents by operating a 24-hour national telephone emergency hotline, **(919) 684-8111** (collect calls are accepted), and helps to increase diver safety awareness through education.

DAN does not maintain any treatment facility nor does it directly provide any form of treatment, but is a service that complements existing medical systems. DAN's most important function is facilitating the entry of the injured diver into the hyperbaric trauma care system by coordinating the efforts of everyone involved in the victim's care.

Calls for routine information that do not concern a suspected diving injury or emergency should be directed to DAN information number (919) 684-2948 from 9 a.m. to 5 p.m. Monday–Friday, Eastern Standard Time. This number should *not* be called for general information of chamber locations. Chamber availability changes periodically making obsolete information dangerous at the time of an emergency. Instead, divers should contact DAN as soon as a diving emergency is suspected.

◄ *The reefs surrounding Desecheo are crowded with colorful sponges and provide plenty of protection for the somewhat shy rock beauty, a member of the angelfish family.*

Hyperbaric treatment and air ambulance service can be costly. All divers who have comprehensive medical insurance should check to make sure that hyperbaric treatment and air ambulance services are adequately covered internationally. DAN membership includes insurance coverage specifically for dive injuries. Four different membership levels offering four different levels of coverage are available.

The *DAN Manual* as well as membership information and applications can be obtained from the Administrative Coordinator, National Diving Alert Network, Duke University Medical Center, Box 3823, Durham, NC 27710.

When the infrequent injury does occur, DAN is prepared to help. DAN support currently comes from diver membership and contributions from the diving industry. It is a legal, nonprofit public service organization and all donations are tax deductible.

Appendix—Dive Operators

This list is included as a service to the reader. The author has made every effort to make this list accurate at the time the book was printed. This list does not constitute an endorsement of these operators and dive shops. If operators/owners wish to be considered for future reprints/editions, please contact Pisces Books, P.O. Box 2608, Houston, Texas 77252-2608.

Aquatica Underwater Adventures
P.O. Box 250350
Ramey, PR 00604
Tel. (809) 890-6071
Fax (809) 890-6071

Arecibo Dive Shop
868 Miramar Ave.
Arecibo, PR 00612
Tel. (809) 880-DIVE

Blue Caribe Dive Center
P.O. Box 1574
Vieques, PR 00765
Tel. (809) 741-2522
Fax (809) 741-1313

Blue Water Scuba
Route 167 Marginal A-14
Bayamon Gardens
Bayamon, PR 00957
Tel. (809) 730-0707
Fax (809) 730-0707

Boqueron Dive Shop
P.O. Box 910
Boqueron, PR 00622
Tel. (809) 851-2155
Fax (809) 851-2155

Calypso Divers
P.O. Box 902
Lajas, PR 00667
Tel. (809) 899-6212
Fax (809) 899-6212

Captain Bill's Dive Shop
HC-01 Box 4181
Rincón, PR 00677
Tel. (809) 823-0390
Fax (809) 823-0390

Caribbean Divers Institute
8-32 Balle Verde
Fajardo, PR 00738
Tel. (809) 860-2177

Caribbean Marine Services
371 Fulladoza
Culebra, PR 00775
Tel. (809) 742-3555
Fax (809) 742-0566

Caribbean School of Aquatics
Taft #1, Apr. 10 S
San Juan, PR 00911
Tel. (809) 723-4740

Caribe Aquatic Adventures
P.O. Box 2470
San Juan, PR 00902-2470
Tel. (809) 724-1882

Coral Head Divers
P.O. Box 10246
Humacao, PR 00792
Tel. (809) 850-7208
Fax (809) 852-6602
800-635-4529

Culebra Dive Shop
P.O. Box 467
Culebra, PR 00775
Tel. (809) 742-0566

Dive Copamarina
P.O. Box 1412
Guanica, PR 00653
Tel. (809) 821-6009
Fax (809) 821-0070

Dorado Marine Center
P.O. Box 705
Dorado, PR 00646
Tel. (809) 796-4645
Fax (809) 796-7323

Fantasy Scuba
Box 2670
Vega Baja, PR 00694
Tel. (809) 858-6371
Fax (809) 858-6371

Gregory's Dive Center
Urb. Ind. San Rafael Lot 9
Center Ponce, PR 00731
Tel. (809) 840-6424
Fax (809) 840-6424

Humacao Diver Service Center
Ave Font Martelo #15
Humacao, PR 00791
Tel. (809) 852-4530
Fax (809) 850-4250

La Cueva Submarina
P.O. Box 151
Isabela, PR 00662
#110 Tel. (809) 872-1094
Fax (809) 872-1094

Marine Sports and Dive Shop
P.O. Box 7711
Ponce, PR 00732
Tel. (809) 844-6175
Fax (809) 844-6175

Mundo Submarino, Inc.
Laguna Gardens Shopping Center
Isla Verde, Carolina, PR 00979
Tel. (809) 791-5764
Fax (809) 791-5764

Ocean Scuba Shop
Calle Dr. Gatell #1
Yauco, PR 00698
Tel. (809) 856-8206

Ocean Sports Inc.
77 Isla Verde
Isla Verde, PR 00979
Tel. (809) 268-2329
Fax (809) 727-3869

Palomino Divers
P.O. Box 70005
Fajardo, PR 00738
Tel. (809) 863-1000
Fax (809) 863-8363
800-468-5228

Parguera Divers
P.O. Box 514
Lajas, PR 00667
Tel. (809) 899-4171
800-359-0747

Professional Dive
P.O. Box 40893
San Juan, PR 00940
Tel. (809) 793-1164
Fax (809) 782-7330

Scuba Centro
Roosevelt Ave. 1156
Puerto Nuevo, PR 00920
Tel. (809) 781-8086

Scuba Connection
Av. Gautier Beniter
Cagusas, PR 00725
Tel. (809) 744-8578

Sea Ventures
P.O. Box 7002
Fajardo, PR 00738
Tel. (809) 863-3483
800-739-3483

South West Scuba
Tel. (809) 833-6455

Index

 **Pisces Books®**

Be sure to check out these other great books from Pisces:

Caribbean Reef Ecology
Great Reefs of the World
Skin Diver Magazine's Book of Fishes, 2nd Edition
Shooting Underwater Video: A Complete Guide to the Equipment and Techniques for Shooting, Editing, and Post-Production
Snorkeling . . . Here's How
Watching Fishes: Understanding Coral Reef Fish Behavior
Watersports Guide to Cancun

Diving and Snorkeling Guides to:

Australia: Coral Sea and Great Barrier Reef
Australia: Southeast Coast and Tasmania
The Bahamas: Family Islands and Grand Bahama
The Bahamas: Nassau and New Providence Island, 2nd Ed.
Bali
Belize
The Best Caribbean Diving
Bonaire
The British Virgin Islands
California's Central Coast
The Cayman Islands, 2nd Ed.
Cozumel, 2nd Ed.
Curaçao
Fiji
Florida's East Coast, 2nd Ed.
The Florida Keys, 2nd Ed.

The Great Lakes
Guam and Yap
The Hawaiian Islands, 2nd Ed.
Jamaica
Northern California and the Monterey Peninsula, 2nd Ed.
The Pacific Northwest
Palau
Puerto Rico
The Red Sea
Roatan and Honduras' Bay Islands
St. Maarten, Saba, and St. Eustatius
Southern California, 2nd Ed.
Texas
Truk Lagoon
The Turks and Caicos Islands
The U.S. Virgin Islands, 2nd Ed.
Vanuatu

Available from your favorite dive shop, bookstore, or directly from the publisher: Pisces Books®, a division of Gulf Publishing Company, Book Division, Dept. AD, P.O. Box 2608, Houston, Texas 77252-2608. (713) 520-4444.

Include purchase price plus $4.95 for shipping and handling. IL, NJ, PA, and TX residents add appropriate tax.